How to Train Your

Cane Corso

Effective Techniques to Smart Socialization Strategies for Caring, Grooming, and Raising an Obedient Guardian Dog

Finnley Crestwood

Disclaimer

The information in this book is intended for general guidance on training. It is not a substitute for professional advice. Always consult with a veterinarian or certified dog trainer for tailored recommendations. The author and publisher disclaim any liability for actions taken based on the content of this book.

Finnley Crestwood
How to Train your
Cane
Corso
BONUS:
20 Cane Corso
dog Homemade
Food Recipes
Effective Techniques to Smart Socialization
Strategies for Caring, Grooming, and Raising an
Obedient Guardian Dog

Contents

Introduction

I cautiously made my way down the dimly lit alley, the only sound being the crunch of my shoes on the gravel, breaking the silence of the night as the flickering lighting cast an ominous shadow. I was bracing myself for whatever lurked in the darkness, my body and mind on high alert. Just over the bend, I caught sight of him—the menacing shape of a burly man standing in my way. I was paralyzed with fear until I noticed the excited waving of the tail and the perked-up ears. "Good boy, Rocco!" My Cane Corso eagerly came running over to say hello, and I let out a breath of relief.

The Cane Corso may look intimidating with its mastiff-like appearance and massive frame, but anyone who has lived with this misunderstood breed knows that beyond their tough exterior lurks a loving soul. Cane Corso, whose name comes from the Latin word "cohorts" meaning "protector," is a devoted family dog that is distrustful of outsiders and maintains an unbreakable tie with its own kind. Cane Corso's ancestry dates back to the Roman Empire when the dog served as both a farm guardian and a hunter of wild boar. Modern Cane Corsos still have strong defensive instincts but are well-loved as loving companions.

As a long-time Cane Corso owner and dog training enthusiast, I'm always awed by this breed's intellect, athleticism, and desire to work in unison with their owner. When properly socialized and managed with positive reinforcement, the Cane Corso becomes a delightfully responsive partner. However, their innate wariness mixed with their significant size and power make extensive training a critical necessity for everyone's safety and enjoyment.

While Cane Corsos with an aggressive temperament are good guard dogs and deterrents, canines chosen for their aggressiveness do no one any good. As with any working breed, ethics and accountability must be the hallmark of all Cane Corso breeding programs and ownership. Early socialization, thorough training, physical exercise, and cooperative decision-making are important to cultivating Cane Corso's best attributes and limiting any bad tendencies.

As the popularity of Cane Corsos expands across the globe, it's crucial that new owners respect the breed's specific needs. The Cane Corso is not for beginner dog owners. They require a firm yet compassionate touch coupled with clear clarification of boundaries. Providing the correct structure, motivation, and outlet for their great drive allows the Cane Corso to thrive as the ideal loving friend.

Within these pages, I share the wealth of insider knowledge I've gathered from years of experience living with Cane Corsos and immersing myself in positive reinforcement dog training techniques.

Consider this book your personal blueprint for selecting, growing, training, and enjoying one of the world's most exquisite protectors - the Cane Corso. While their appearance whispers "beware", good handling transforms the Cane Corso into a faithful best friend. Let's go on your trip together...

Chapter One

Introducing the Cane Corso

History and Origins of the Breed

The Cane Corso is a huge Italian breed of mastiff that has historical roots as a multipurpose farm guarding and hunting dog. Tracing back to ancient Roman times, the Cane Corso benefited farmers in driving livestock and swine, while also serving as a proficient hunter of wild boar. Their name stems from the Latin "cohorts" meaning "protector" or "guardian of the farmyard".

During the Middle Ages, the Cane Corso continued to serve as an indispensable farm dog in Italy, notably in the rural countryside of Southern Italy. They secured property, handled cattle, hunted game, and safeguarded families from thieves and robbers along lonely farmsteads. Their intimidating stature and imposing presence prevented wrongdoers.

In the 19th and 20th centuries, Cane Corsos nearly faced extinction due to a dwindling necessity for farmyard security dogs and hunters. However, enthusiasts in Italy sought to resurrect the breed in the 1970s, utilizing pups from distant rural areas that nearly matched the original working Cane Corso. These restoration efforts resulted in recognition by major kennel clubs in the 1980s and 1990s.

Today's Cane Corso retains much of its ancestral instincts as a guardian and hunter. While no longer employed to move cattle, its protective temperament makes it an ideal watchdog. Early socialization and training are needed to promote this breed's greatest features while limiting undesired hostility. When properly reared, the Cane Corso bonds very closely with its family members.

In appearance, the Cane Corso is a huge, muscular, and imposing dog that expresses power and athleticism. It normally stands 25-27 inches tall and weighs 90-120 pounds when fully grown. The Cane Corso features a large head, floppy ears that can be clipped, and a docked or natural tail. Its short coat comes in shades of black, gray, fawn, or red. The Cane Corso moves with a confident, yet accessible gait.

While the Cane Corso nearly perished in the mid-20th century, determined Italian breeders were able to bring it back from the brink of extinction. Today, it gets recognition from all major kennel associations and has a growing following across the world as an excellent companion dog and guardian. With proper care and training, the Cane Corso maintains its standing as a versatile and imposing Italian breed.

Typical Temperament and Personality

The Cane Corso is an amazing Italian breed that builds strong relationships with family but remains a little aloof and distrustful of strangers. While their menacing appearance can be off-putting, Cane Corsos are dedicated and friendly with their own owners when properly socialized and treated. Here's an overview of the Cane Corso's typical temperament:

Loyal and Bonds Closely with Family

The most defining attribute of the Cane Corso is its unshakable loyalty and commitment to its family. This is a breed that ties very strongly with owners and is protective of family members, especially children. With proper introduction, Cane Corsos become compassionate friends and "nanny dogs" that watch over kids. Their tight relationship also renders them prone to separation anxiety when left alone for long periods. Proper crate training and separation practices should be implemented from puppyhood.

Wary of Strangers

While highly loyal to the family, the Cane Corso is inherently distrustful of unknown individuals entering its area. This wariness ties back to their history as fearsome guard dogs on Italian farms. Cane Corsos will employ their frightening bark and imposing presence to repel outsiders or intruders. This protective instinct makes them ideal watchdogs, but also requires thorough socialization from an early age to prevent excessive aggressiveness.

Confident and Powerful

As a huge, powerful breed created for managing cattle and wild boar, the Cane Corso emanates power and confidence. This is a bold and proud dog that carries itself with dignity. Cane Corsos have a high level of self-assuredness and are not timid or shy. However, they are also sophisticated enough to recognize when to demonstrate restraint and tranquility, once properly educated.

Athletic and Active

The Cane Corso needs frequent movement and exercise to channel its innate athleticism and vitality. Whether patrolling the limits of its property or playing a game of fetch, this breed thrives when provided daily outlets for activity. Without adequate movement, the Cane Corso may grow frustrated or develop undesired behaviors. Providing the correct amount of exercise and mental stimulation is crucial.

Reasonably Calm Indoors

Despite its imposing size and protective instincts, the Cane Corso tends to be rather calm and collected when indoors around its family. This breed settles quietly indoors and works well in homes, provided its exercise needs are met. The Cane Corso is not inherently hyperactive and will be comfortable reclining with its owners rather than pacing or acting uptight. A stimulating walk or play session lets this breed relax nicely for snuggle time.

Requires Early, Consistent Training

This huge, strong breed needs significant socialization and obedience training starting from puppyhood. With the correct training method, the Cane Corso becomes a fantastic companion. Without adequate handling, this breed might become too protective or attempt to exert authority. Early socialization avoids undue wariness, while obedience training creates critical boundaries.

Not For Novice Owners

First-time or timid owners may find the Cane Corso's big size, protective instincts, and power difficult to control. This breed works best with experienced owners who position themselves as clear authority figures. The Cane Corso needs a firm but caring hand along with patient but constant training. This minimizes stubbornness while promoting the breed's strongest attributes of devotion and companionship.

Considerations Before Getting a Cane Corso

The Cane Corso is a wonderful breed for many owners, but it comes with particular considerations and requirements. Before deciding if this robust Italian breed is the ideal choice, here are some crucial points to consider:

Activity Level Cane Corsos need daily outlets for their immense energy, whether lengthy walks, runs, or active play sessions. A Cane Corso left sedentary and under-exercised may become frustrated and develop undesired behaviors. This breed thrives with owners who like hiking, jogging, swimming, or indulging in canine sports. The Cane Corso is not suited for primarily sedentary owners. Be prepared to provide at least 60-90 minutes of daily activities.

Training Commitment

This confident, strong-minded breed requires significant obedience training from puppyhood through maturity to manage its guarding instincts and might. Cane Corso puppies should participate in formal obedience training to socialize appropriately with other dogs and practice commands under distraction. Intermediate and advanced instruction should continue throughout maturity along with frequent repetition of commands at home. Training is a lifetime commitment for this breed.

Grooming Needs

The Cane Corso's short coat requires only occasional brushing and minimal maintenance overall. However, their shedding can be considerable, especially during seasonal shifts. This breed is not hypoallergenic and sheds more than some other breeds. Be prepared for dog hair on furniture, carpet, and clothing. Investing in deshedding tools can help reduce loose hair.

Supervision Around Other Animals

With adequate socialization and training, Cane Corsos may adjust to homes with other pets. However, their intense prey instinct means they may regard cats, rabbits, or small dogs as a quarry until trained otherwise. Close supervision is essential around smaller animals. Cane Corsos can be territorial of food/toys around other dogs. Proper "leave it" and "drop" cues should be stressed.

Wariness of Strangers

The protective Cane Corso utilizes its frightening bark and imposing presence to keep outsiders away from its family and territory. This makes the species a superb watchdog but necessitates prudence around new visitors. Guests should be appropriately presented on neutral territory like outdoors. Obedience commands like "sit" or "stay" can soothe the dog during interactions.

Special Precautions Around Children

Cane Corsos can flourish in families with children, although care must be taken considering the breed's size and guarding tendencies. Proper socialization and training should adapt the Cane Corso to acceptable, gentle conduct with kids. Children must be taught how to safely engage with the dog to avoid potential accidents. Unmonitored play time is unwise until the Cane Corso fully matures.

Potential Dog Aggression

Cane Corsos may demonstrate canine aggression toward strange dogs of the same sex, given their guarding ancestry. They should not visit dog parks. Multi-dog homes may be hard depending on context. Socialization from puppyhood is crucial. Owners should be prepared to intervene during interactions on walks and offer proper obedience training.

Barking Tendencies

This loud breed tends to bark at anything considered out of the ordinary, including strangers near their homes or unexpected sounds at night. Drive-by barking can become an unwanted habit without adequate training. Teaching the "quiet" cue and giving appropriate activity/companionship can help stop excessive barking.

Strong Prey Drive

As descendants of mastiffs used for hunting boar, Cane Corsos retain a powerful prey drive. This makes them unsuitable homes with smaller pets like rabbits, guinea pigs, birds, or cats unless properly desensitized to these animals through diligent training from early puppyhood. Owners must be prepared to constantly supervise and intervene to override chasing instincts.

The safest approach is to avoid adopting a Cane Corso into a multi-pet household containing any small animals that could trigger predatory reactions. This breed should not be left unmonitored with potential "prey" under any circumstances. Proper management of the Cane Corso's strong prey drive is essential for harmonious relations.

Chapter Two

Getting Ready for Your New Cane Corso Puppies

Making Your House Puppy-Friendly

If you're looking to welcome an active Cane Corso puppy into your home, you'll need to make some changes. In preparation for welcoming this huge and active breed into your home, consider the following advice:

Eliminate Dangers and Pollutants

To see the inside of a building from a puppy's point of view, get down on all fours. Things like houseplants, medicines, cables, small objects, and anything that could be bitten or eaten should be removed. Puppy raids on trash cans are common, so it's best to keep them out of reach.

Safeguard Unstable Items

For fun, puppies will playfully pull, tug, and bump into things. To secure any unstable furniture like bookcases so they don't tip over if used as climbing structures. Also, fasten rugs to the floor so they don't slide. Top-heavy goods should be transferred to sturdier low tables or storage.

Block Off Certain Rooms/Areas

Use baby gates to prevent entrance to rooms like kitchens or bedrooms where a puppy could get into mischief or danger. Make sure the gates are high and solid, since Cane Corsos may readily scale or knock down feeble barriers. You want to confine access until house training is fully established.

Remove Tempting Items from Reach

Put away enticing items that may trigger interest or guarding behavior in your Cane Corso puppy. This contains children's toys, shoes, bills, trash, food dishes, and high-value snacks. Until you have control, avoid leaving anything within reach that may be chewed up, swallowed, or battled over.

Adjust Cords and Hide Wires

Puppies are fascinated by electrical cables, which can cause electrocution or burns if eaten. Tape down, cover, or encapsulate any stray wires. Restrict access behind TVs and computer equipment. Consider cordless window treatments to remove dangling cords altogether.

Inspect the Yard for Safety

Walk your entire property to detect and fix any hazards in the yard, such as hazardous plants, sharp equipment, chemicals, or gaps in fencing. Your curious dog will enthusiastically explore the yard, so you want to ensure it's a secure zone. Consider installing a dig barrier around the perimeter if your dog is tempted to escape by digging.

Dog-Proof Garbage Cans

Invest in dog-proof garbage cans with locking lids and store them in cupboards or closets. Alternatively, you can use kid locks or bungee cords to fasten lids. Ingenious pups are adept at overturning unsecured garbage containers for delectable tidbits. Remove temptation altogether till training advances.

Create a Puppy Playroom

Set up a designated puppy play area with toys to engage your Corso when you can't actively supervise their wandering. This safe, engaging place should have chew toys, puzzle toys, and a cozy crate stocked with food. Provide fresh water availability as well. Rotate toys to keep your pooch entertained.

Cover Furniture and Carpets

Protect your furnishings from puppy messes with washable coverings or old sheets. You want to lessen frustration over regular puppy mistakes. Designate sections with tile, wood, or easy-clean flooring for early home alone time. Let your Corso progressively earn access to carpeted spaces.

Establish a Feeding Station

Select an out-of-the-way place to act as a designated feeding area for your pet. This will teach them that food only comes from that precise bowl in that particular area. Feed on a mat that catches dropped food and water. Restrict access during mealtimes until your puppy has a good "leave it" command.

Puppy Proof Doors and Windows

Use self-closing systems on doors going outside to prevent darts and escapes. Make sure your yard is properly secured with no gaps. For windows, consider locks or barriers to keep your dog from climbing through screens or falling out of open windows after they learn to put paws up on the sills. Prevention is crucial.

Gathering Supplies

Preparing for a Cane Corso puppy entails acquiring crucial goods to assist train, feed, and caring for your new addition. Stock up on these things before taking home your bouncy ball of fur:

For Containment and Sleep:
- Sturdy container with a divider panel to alter the size as your Corso grows
- Baby gates to block staircases and rooms

- Outdoor kennel or run during periods of outdoor captivity

For Identification and Health:
- Flat buckle collar and ID tag inscribed with contact info
- Leash ideal for large, robust dogs
- Microchip and registration paperwork
- Veterinarian details and vaccination/exam schedule

For Potty Training:
- Leash for taking the puppy outside often
- Enzyme-based cleanser for accident clean-up
- Treats for outside potty success
- Bell to hang by door and train pup to ring

For Feeding:
- Stainless steel dishes for meals and water
- High-grade dog food ideal for large breeds
- Automatic waterer to keep water fresh

For Chewing:

- Variety of chew toys like Kongs, ropes, and natural bones
- Nylabones, Benebones, or other sturdy chew goods
- Enzymatic chews for teething relief
- Interactive food puzzle toys

For Grooming:

- Pin brush and de-shedding tool for coat maintenance
- Nail clippers appropriate for large dogs
- Ear cleanser and cotton balls
- Dog-formulated shampoo/conditioner

For Training:

- Clicker, cookies, and pouch for positive reinforcement
- Obedience class enrollment form
- Muzzles to make pup familiar with handling
- Interactive tug and fetch toys for play incentives

For Travel:

- Sturdy crate that can be secured in cars

- Seatbelt harness to restrain dog safely in automobile

- Non-spill water bottle and collapsible bowl

For Cleanliness:

- Pet stain/odor remover for accident clean-up

- Dog-safe disinfectant wipes for paws and surfaces

- Shedding control tools like shedding blade

- Odor-removing sprays/candles for the house

For First Aid:

- Basic first aid kit with gauze, bandages, sticky tape

- Antiseptic wipes and hydrogen peroxide

- Instant cold compress packets

- Eyewash solution

- LED safety light collar

Finding a Reputable Breeder or Rescue

Where you purchase your Cane Corso puppy is a tremendously important decision with long-term consequences on health, temperament, and training. Take time to explore these options:

AKC Breeders

The optimum source is frequently a breeder registered with the American Kennel Club's Bred with HEART program. These breeders promise health testing, temperament screening, appropriate breeding techniques, and AKC certification. Ask to see OFA certifications, meet parent dogs, and inspect house circumstances.

Health Screenings

Reputable breeders examine breeding dogs for disorders common in Cane Corsos including hip/elbow dysplasia, ocular abnormalities, cardiac problems, and autoimmune thyroiditis. They provide OFA certificates for hips, elbows, and thyroid. Expect health assurances.

Temperament Testing

Ethical Cane Corso breeders also temperament test mature dogs by examining reactions to strangers, odd settings, youngsters, and loud noises. Nervous, acute, or extremely aggressive temperaments should reject breeding candidates. Look for steady, confident personalities.

Socialization and Enrichment

Quality breeders correctly socialize Cane Corso puppies by gradually introducing new sights, sounds, people, and experiences in a favorable manner. The surroundings should give different enrichment through toys, games, and outings. The adjustment to new residences is easier.

Clean Conditions

The breeder's home and kennel should be clean, large, and sanitary. While scents are expected with several dogs, intolerable aromas, small confined cages, and filthy water bowls are red flags. Seek out humane conditions.

Wait for Lists and Screening

Top breeders rigorously evaluate applicants and establish wait lists for their puppies. Expect to answer questions about your home, lifestyle, and abilities to teach a guardian breed. Reliable breeders want to ensure their pups get to suitable lifelong homes.

Contracts and Documentation

A respectable breeder gives documents on pedigree, microchipping, deworming/vaccinations, health testing of parents, care instructions, and continuous support. A contract protects both parties. Avoid any breeder who does not offer documentation.

Rescues and Shelters

Many gorgeous Cane Corso dogs need homes through specialized rescues and shelters. Adopting minimizes support of puppy mills. Have realistic expectations about training needs. Seek rescues that temperament screen and match each dog with appropriate homes.

Adult vs. Puppy

Consider adopting an adult Cane Corso (over age 1) if you feel overwhelmed by puppy training requirements. Adult rescues let you bypass potty training and enjoy a calmer attitude after the puppy stage has passed.

Patience and Flexibility

With rescues, background details may be limited and behavioral issues more prevalent from past neglect or abuse. Adopters should demonstrate patience and flexibility in dealing with potential fearfulness, reactivity, or separation anxiety. However, proper training and environmental management can help many issues improve. The rewards of providing a second chance to a rescued Cane Corso make the extra effort worthwhile.

Chapter Three

Bringing Home Your Cane Corso Puppy

Preparing for the First Day and Night

The arrival of your Cane Corso puppy is a joyful event! Proper planning will help ease the adjustment and set you both up for success. Follow these tips while taking home your puppy:

Puppy-Proof Your Home

In the days before your dog arrives, evaluate your home room-by-room and puppy-proof any threats. Remove loose items that could be swallowed or knocked over. Restrict entry to non-puppy-safe areas. Ensure your yard is properly fenced with no gaps.

Gather Supplies

Stock up on essentials like a collar, leash, ID tag, food/water bowls, dog food, toys, treats, cleaning materials, and a nice crate. Having all gear ready ensures you can focus totally on your pup when they reach home.

Schedule Time Off Work

If possible, take a few days off when first bringing home your dog. This allows you to focus on helping them adjust without job disruptions. If you can't take time off, inquire if a friend or family member can puppysit for the first few days.

Establish a Routine

Follow a consistent schedule for meals, walking, playtime, training sessions, and crated nap times. This promotes a natural rhythm and supports housetraining attempts. Routines make dogs feel secure.

Set Up a Safe Space

Create an enclosed, comforting environment like a pen or small room where your puppy can settle in those first days home. Limiting access minimizes accidents and destructive chewing while your puppy adjusts. Provide fresh water, toys, pads, and a crate for rest.

Practice Crate Introduction

In advance of pickup day, introduce crates with food and praise so it becomes a joyful refuge. Bring a familiar, unwashed blanket from the breeder to ease acclimation.

Choose a Low-Key First Day

Keep early encounters and stimuli low-key to prevent overloading your puppy. Let them sniff and explore your home and yard at their own calm pace. Save high-activity play till after an adjustment period.

Take Them Out Frequently

Prevent accidents by putting your puppy outside to potty often - at least every 2 hours while roaming and 30 minutes after eating, playing, or waking up. Praise and treat toilet success outside. Clean any indoor accidents thoroughly with an enzymatic cleanser.

Monitor Closely

Directly oversee all investigations and play sessions - don't rely on baby gates alone. Puppies are very quick and can slip into holes you wouldn't expect. Close doors to non-puppy zones.

Practice Obedience Basics

Use delectable treats to encourage habits like coming when called, basic leash etiquette, and tricks like "sit". Keep sessions quick and lively. End on a positive note.

Get Familiar with Signals

Learn your puppy's particular indicators for wanting to pee/poop including circling, sniffing, and squatting - so you can get them outside ASAP after giving signals. Preventing indoor mess creates healthy behaviors.

Say Goodbye to Carpet

Expect spills on the carpet and rugs initially. Nature's Miracle cleanser neutralizes odors. Use baby gates to restrict access until potty training advances. Confine time on the carpet till you have better control.

Prepare for an Active Night

The first night might be lively and unpleasant as puppies whine and bark while adjusting to new surroundings. Provide plush toys for comfort and let them tire themselves out safely in the crate.

Potty Before Bed

Take your puppy out promptly before bedtime to ensure an empty bladder and intestines overnight. Praise for finishing business outside, then settle them inside the crate with a treat and blanket.

Respond Quickly to Night Waking

If overnight whining or restlessness arises, take your pup out for a boring pee excursion on a leash, then right back in the crate with minimum fuss. Gradually, they will sleep through the night.

Housetraining Fundamentals

Successfully housetraining your Cane Corso puppy demands monitoring, patience, and a proactive approach. Here are key ideas for tackling potty training:

Establish a Routine

Adhere to a consistent daily plan for waking, feeding, playing, training, and putting your puppy outside. Regular routines foster predictability in bathroom behaviors so your puppy learns to hold it between periods.

Frequent Outings

Take your puppy outside frequently, at least every two hours plus soon after naps, meals, playtime, and first thing in the morning. Puppies have small bladders and inadequate control. Frequent outings avoid mishaps indoors.

Keep Trips Boring

When you take your puppy outside, keep the outings quiet and business-like. Simply walk to the intended potty site, wait while leashed, then praise and reward with treats for going to the appropriate place. End outings immediately afterward.

Choose a Potty Spot

Initially stick to one specific outdoor toilet area instead of letting your pooch explore and get distracted. Going in a constant area helps build a habit. As training advances, you can add other permitted venues.

Reward Success

The second your puppy finishes their business outside, passionately praise and distribute high-value rewards. This reinforces the desired behavior. Your pup will make the link that pottying outdoors is incredibly rewarding.

Limit Access Indoors

When you can't immediately oversee your puppy, restrict access to rooms indoors using baby gates or crates. The more opportunities you can remove for stealthy inside accidents, the faster your dog will learn.

Catch Mistakes in the Act

If you catch your puppy in the act of an indoor accident, swiftly intervene with a forceful "ah ah!" Then promptly accompany them outside to finish.

Praise for completing outside. Limit scolding though - it can postpone house training.

Respond to Sniffing and Circling

Learn to recognize your puppy's pee cues like circling, abruptly stopping to sniff, or heading to corners. These indicators mean toilet time is near, so hurry outdoors immediately away before any accidents arise.

Supervise Rigorously

Directly supervise your puppy while they are unrestrained in your home during the house training process. Don't simply listen for noises - monitor them like a hawk for indicators they need to go out. Prevention is crucial.

Thorough Cleanup

Promptly clean all indoor accidents with an enzymatic pet odor neutralizer. Dog noses are incredibly sensitive, so any remaining aroma will encourage recurrent accidents in the same location.

Allow No Exceptions

Stick to your housetraining practices consistently. Make sure all family members implement the same rules. No gaps in taking the puppy out frequently or praising outside potty. Consistency is key.

Troubleshoot Setbacks

Accidents and setbacks are normal throughout training. If they persist, rule out medical reasons, then assess your approach. Increase supervision, take outside more frequently, widen confinement when you can't observe closely, and review diet.

Be Patient!

Housetraining takes several weeks and months for a young puppy to fully learn. There will be ups and downs. Stick to a positive training strategy, enhance prevention, and recognize minor successes along the way.

Crate Training Basics

Introducing your Cane Corso puppy to a crate establishes a vital tool for safety, house training, and behavior management. Follow these guidelines for effective crate training:

Select the Right Crate

Choose an adult-sized container that will accommodate your Cane Corso when fully matured. Include a dividing panel to adjust interior space as your pet grows. Ensure it is strong and secure.

Make the Crate Welcoming

Place a nice blanket and favorite toys in the crate to create a comfortable den. Sprinkling biscuits or a food-stuffed Kong inside inspires your puppy to enter voluntarily and associate the crate with nice things.

Take It Slow at First

Begin crate training gradually. Reward your pup with treats for brief moments lounging in the open crate. Build up duration very carefully to prevent overwhelming them initially. Work at your pup's speed.

Create Positive Associations

Request your puppy to enter the crate using a cue like "kennel up" followed by a food treat reward. Offer praised meals in the container. Randomly give high-value chews inside the package to build delight.

Use the Crate in Daily Life

Incorporate the crate naturally into your puppy's daily schedule for naps, quiet time, mealtimes, and safe downtime when you're occupied. Making it a regular part of life minimizes dread.

Practice Separation

Gradually increase alone time in the crate with separation exercises. Give a puzzling toy, exit briefly, return, and reward serenity. Increase your absence very gradually, paying alert to any signs of concern.

Always Reward Calmness

Make an effort to allow your puppy out of the kennel only when calm and settled. This teaches them that a calm demeanor allows egress while barking and fussing keeps the door shut.

Here is the continuation of the crate training section:

Prevent Traumatic Exits

Never forcefully remove a terrified, agitated, or stubborn puppy from their crate. This can produce unfavorable associations. Instead, patiently promote calm conduct and coax them out with praise and treats.

Ignore Protests

Expect vocal objections and grumbling during early crate training. As long as your puppy's requirements are addressed, disregard the protests. Release and reward only quiet stillness to shape the desired behavior.

Use for Naps

Enforce naps in the crate to teach your energetic puppy to settle on cue and prevent over-tiredness. One to two hours in the crate followed by potty and playtime can prevent crankiness.

Nighttime Crating

Luxurious, large containers are great for the evening. Place the crate in your bedroom initially so your puppy feels reassured by your presence. You can move it once they transition well.

Troubleshoot Crying

If sobbing during crate time occurs, consider whether the crate is too big (condensed space), needs more enrichment, or requires desensitization through separation training and rewarding silence.

Use Safely

Check that your puppy can sit and stand comfortably in their box. Remove collars that can snag and ensure you shut the door properly. Never use crates for punishment or excessive imprisonment.

Crate Restlessly?

If your puppy seems uncomfortable or anxious in the crate howling, barking, or pawing wildly, you may be progressing too soon. Slow down the introduction and make the crate more pleasurable. Consult a trainer if concerns continue.

The Crate for Life

Properly introduced crates continue offering safety and comfort throughout your Cane Corso's adulthood. Dogs naturally seek den-like sanctuaries to feel secure in their environment. The container becomes a lifelong haven.

Chapter Four

Socializing Your Cane Corso Puppy

Introducing New People

Early socialization is crucial for the naturally wary Cane Corso. Carefully exposing your dog to new people in a pleasant manner helps avoid unjustified hostility and overprotective impulses from forming. Follow these tips:

Start Young

Begin introducing your Cane Corso to new individuals right immediately in the first few months of life. Early favorable exposures help shape sociability at critical imprinting times. Maintain this socialization steadily as your dog matures.

Go Slowly

Don't overwhelm your puppy by introducing multiple new individuals all at once initially. Start with just one or two new individuals at a time for brief sessions, providing adequate praise and treats for respectful behavior. Gradually increase interactions.

Pay Attention to Body Language

Watch your puppy's body language intently during introductions. If they seem tight, worried, afraid, or overstimulated, tone down the interactions and keep them brief and positive. Don't flood with too much too quickly.

Have Guests Ignore

Instruct guests to entirely ignore your puppy at first - no direct eye contact or petting. Have appetizing goodies ready. Once the dog settles, the guest can softly administer treats while praising in a calm, friendly tone. This teaches good associations.

Start Outside the Home

Initial interactions will go smoothly on neutral territory outside your home, which your dog may guard. A park, patio, or walkway minimizes territoriality. After repeated neutral meetings, proceed to home introductions.

Keep Leashed Initially

Keep your puppy on a leash and harness during early introductions so you can readily redirect any jumping or nipping behavior. As social skills improve, your pup can progress to off-leash greetings.

Discourage Jumping

If your puppy leaps on newcomers, divert this behavior quickly by drawing their focus back to you with a treat. Ask the person to turn away from jumping. Have them welcome your puppy only once all four paws are on the floor.

Steady Exposure

Aim to introduce your Cane Corso to a wide variety of people - all ages, appearances, voices, and actions (within reason). This inhibits interpreting specific individuals like youngsters, men with hats, or yelling kids as scary. Variety is vital.

Handle Touching

Desensitize your puppy to handling and affection by unexpected persons like vets. Make sure people approach touch softly from behind your puppy's chin rather than reaching over their head, which might feel dangerous.

Respect Fear Periods

Socialization may hit difficult patches during developmental fear periods at 9-10 weeks and 6-14 months. Ease up if your puppy seems scared and provide only calm, positive exposures. Pushing too hard can backfire.

Enroll in Puppy Classes

A fantastic option for safe off-leash socializing is supervised puppy courses. Look for positive reinforcement-based classes. Check vaccination needs and avoid classes with violent puppies.

Monitor Dog Interactions

Supervise all puppy play sessions carefully to prevent bullying or aggressive habits from arising. Correct inappropriate actions like mounting quickly. Interrupt play regularly to check in with your pet.

End on a Positive Note

After an introduction session, make sure the last interaction is pleasant and relaxed, with rewards and praise. No scared reactions lingering. Keep interaction sessions brief enough to minimize overstimulation.

Getting Used to Other Animals

Cane Corsos have great impulses to chase and seize creatures that flee. With proper training, they can adjust to homes with other pets. Follow this guidance:

Start Young

Begin regulated socialization with calm, sociable animals right away in puppyhood. Early, consistent good interactions will shape your Cane Corso's comfort levels around other pets versus considering them as prey.

Use Leashes and Gates

Keep early introductions on-leash, behind baby gates, or with crates separating the animals. This allows for progressive exposure in controlled conditions that set everyone up for success.

Reward Calm Behavior

When your puppy remains calm and relaxed with other animals, deliver eager praise and high-value food incentives. Correct any lunging, barking, or chasing with redirects. You want to actively reinforce courteous behavior, not over-arousal.

Limit Access

Don't leave your Cane Corso puppy alone unsupervised with existing pets throughout the acclimatization phase. Use gates, crates, and leashes to manage interactions until you witness consistent compassion from the puppy.

Respect Fearful Animals

Some creatures are cautious by nature. If your other dogs seem overwhelmed or terrified of the new puppy, offer them breaks from contact in a separate room or box until they acquire confidence.

Provide Escape Routes

Smaller pets will gain assurance if you position furniture and fences to give simple "escape routes" away from the puppy as needed. Having exits prevents feeling confined and hunted.

Redirect Interest

If your pooch gets hooked on stalking a cat or pursuing a small dog, halt the action and shift their attention to a toy or food. Then praise for focusing on you. Redirection is powerful.

Model Calm Behavior

Set the tone with your own enthusiasm. If you stiffen up or yell during multi-pet situations, it might ratchet up arousal. Model relaxed, patient energy and talk in quiet tones to impact your puppy's temperament.

Enlist Helpers

It can be useful to expose your Cane Corso puppy to other calm, friendly dogs that can "mentor" appropriate play style and greeting etiquette against impolite or chase-based engagement. Select role models carefully.

Address Problem Reactions

If your puppy demonstrates highly reactive, aggressive, or predatory behavior toward other pets that persists despite training efforts, visit an expert trainer or behaviorist for specialized help.

Prevent Bullying

Some puppies, especially in multi-dog situations, may try to intimidate or impose authority over subservient older canines. Watch attentively for bullying and correct immediately to avoid confrontation and fear.

Be Realistic

In rare situations, a Cane Corso and small pets like rabbits or birds just may not be compatible housemates. If major predatory behavior persists despite considerable training, be realistic about maintaining a safe, happy environment.

Exposing to New Places and Situations

To have a well-adjusted Cane Corso partner, it's vital to introduce your puppy to a wide variety of different places, situations, surfaces, sights, and sounds. Follow this guidance:

Visit New Places

Bring your puppy on regular outings to see new situations like passing buses, crowded parks, or pet stores starting at an early age. Move closer gradually as comfort levels allow while rewarding stillness.

Socialize to Urban Life

If you live in an urban location, expose your puppy often to city sounds like sirens, construction noise, crowds, and public transit. The more various stimuli introduced early on, the better.

Experience Vehicles

Help your Cane Corso puppy get comfortable riding in automobiles by taking them on frequent short car rides to enjoyable areas for walks and play. Introduce crated travel gradually.

Include Some Surfaces

Get your pooch accustomed to walking on a variety of surfaces such as wood floors, tile, grass, gravel, puddles, and metal grates. Touching and movement sensations can initially seem threatening without exposure. Offer snacks on the new surfaces.

Respect Motion Sensitivity

Some Cane Corso puppies may be scared of movements like bicycles, skateboards, or escalators.

Approach things carefully, allowing your puppy to decide the pace. Go slowly and provide praise and treats for interacting with the motion.

Noise Desensitization

Play recordings of sounds like thunderstorms, fireworks, or crowds at a very low intensity during play to desensitize your dog and make startling stimuli seem less scary through counterconditioning.

Mask Scary Sounds

Try disguising potentially scary sounds with soothing background noise. For example, play music to lessen the sound of explosions and provide rewards when any distant booms occur. This establishes favorable connections with the muted noise.

Acknowledge Reactions

Remain cool and use a joyful voice if your puppy seems spooked by new stimuli. Don't coddle them, but offer enthusiastic praise coupled with treats for focusing on you instead of the fear source.

Avoid Overwhelm

It's crucial not to overload your puppy with too many dramatic new experiences at once. Watch their comfort level and don't surpass their ability to take stimuli in stride without becoming afraid.

Carry Treats Always

Keep ready goodies on walks and outings to reward desired responses. For example, give incentives for peaceful check-ins with you around environmental stressors that would ordinarily make your dog nervous or reactive.

Set Them Up for Success

Start new exposures at a comfortable distance where your puppy notices but doesn't respond to a potential stressor like another dog. Reward calm focus on you. Gradually decrease the distance over numerous sessions.

Train Handling

Desensitize your dog to being examined by handling paws, ears, tail, and lips softly while offering rewards. This prepares them for handling by vets and groomers.

End on a Positive Note

When introducing something new or potentially terrifying, make sure your puppy experiences something nice shortly afterward, such as play or rewards, so the stimulus gets associated at least partly positively.

Chapter Five

Basic Training and Obedience for Cane Corsos

Teaching Basic Cues Like Sit, Stay, Come

Mastering basic obedience skills like sit, stay, and come lays the all-important foundation for more advanced training. Follow these tips for teaching core cues:

Sit:

- Hold a treat at your puppy's nose level and slowly move it upwards and back toward their tail as you say "Sit." Their head will tilt up to follow the treat, resulting in their hind end lowering into a seat.

- Use the treat to guide their nose up and back in an arc to fully sit if needed. Mark and reward the moment their butt hits the ground.

- Once your puppy understands following the lure, start saying "sit" first before showing the treat. Provide the reward after they perform the cued behavior.

- Practice in various locations and with light distractions present to strengthen the cue's reliability. Give bonus treats for solid sits when environmental stimuli are present.

Stay:

- After your puppy reliably sits on cue, start asking for short "stay" durations of 2-3 seconds before rewarding with an excited "good stay!" and treat delivery.

- Gradually increase the time interval for the stay up to 30+ seconds, randomly reinforcing with rewards.

- Reinforce movement restraint by rewarding if your puppy remains sitting despite tempting triggers like bouncing balls, opening doors, or nearby playing.

- If your puppy breaks the stay, say "ah ah", guide them back into a sit, and try for a shorter interval again. Keep sessions upbeat using positive methods.

Come:

- Start "come" training on a retractable leash and have a helper feed your puppy a steady stream of tasty treats anytime they move toward you from a short distance away.

- Say your puppy's name excitedly followed by "Come!" to capture their attention. Praise enthusiastically when they reach you for a reward.

- Increase the recall difficulty very gradually by adding more distance, mild distractions, and practicing off-leash in enclosed areas.

- Make sure 9 out of 10 recalls result in an amazing reward party. For any failures, simply go to your puppy instead of repeating cues so coming always pays off.

Leash Training

Teaching loose leash walking prevents pulling and ensures enjoyable walks with your powerful Cane Corso. Follow these tips:

- Start leash training as early as possible in a low-distraction environment like your home or yard.

- Hold tasty treats by your side and walk forward, rewarding when your puppy chooses to walk near your leg looking up for a treat. The leash should drape in a "J" shape.

- Change directions frequently so your puppy learns to follow your movement versus forging ahead. Reward each automatic turn toward you.

- Use high-value life rewards like allowing sniff time or greeting people for focused heeling. This builds drive to stay close.

- If your puppy surges ahead, firmly say "Let's go" and walk the opposite way. Resist leash pulling.

- Practice patiently pausing whenever your puppy hits the end of the leash until the leash slackens. Then proceed forward.

- Work gradually up to sustained healing for longer durations, around corners, speed changes, and mild distractions. Frequently reinforce attention.

- If your puppy starts reacting to triggers like other dogs or people, get their focus back with an exciting "watch" cue, treating when eye contact shifts to you.

- Help your puppy generalize by frequently changing locations for training, and building up to highly distracting areas like pet stores or parks. Have them check in and refocus on you in each place before proceeding.

- Make training upbeat and fun! End each session on a positive note so your puppy enjoys training walks versus being corrected constantly.

- Be patient and persistent. Excellent leash manners take time and consistency. But putting in the upfront work leads to great results!

Managing Jumping and Nipping

Jumping and nipping are common but undesirable behaviors in exuberant Cane Corso puppies that require early guidance:

Prevent Jumping:

- Promptly turn away and fold your arms whenever your puppy jumps up, withholding any attention. Only pet gently with four paws on the floor.

- Ask guests to also avoid facing, touching, or verbally interacting with a jumping puppy. Require polite, settled greetings first.

- Redirect your pup's energy into a "sit" when visitors arrive and reward calm behavior. This prevents leaping.

- Avoid holding your puppy's paws in the air to dance or petting them when they jump. This inadvertently reinforces the behavior.

- Teach incompatible behavior like training them to go to their bed or crate when guests enter until calmer.

- Use leashes during initial greetings to gently restrain jumps while rewarding non-jumpy responses.

Discourage Nipping:

- Say "ouch!" in a high-pitched tone when puppy teeth make contact. Immediately stand up to stop play and ignore them briefly. This teaches biting ends fun.

- Provide appropriate chew toys and redirect any mouthing onto toys instead of hands/clothing. Praise the puppy for using toys properly.

- Avoid wrestling games and over-stimulating puppy play that riles them up into a nippy frenzy. Learning to be gentle is key.

- Teach the puppy to ease up on pressure by briefly holding their mouth closed and stopping play anytime bites exceed gentle mouthing pressure.

- Ensure the puppy gets ample rest and downtime. Overtired puppies are prone to frantic hyper behavior including biting. Enforce naptimes.

- Withhold further play and attention when biting persists until the puppy has settled down. Reward calm, gentle play.

- Offer chew toys or frozen Kongs when your puppy seems to be teething heavily. Soothing cold pressure eases sore gums.

- Consult a trainer or veterinary behaviorist if biting remains problematic after diligently following positive, consistent redirection methods.

Patience and preventing undesirable habits through management are key. The more you reinforce gentle play and discourage overly rough interaction, the better your pup will learn good bite inhibition. Making the right choices is rewarding!

Chapter Six

Advanced Obedience and Commands

Teaching Heel, Wait, Leave It

Once your Cane Corso puppy knows fundamental commands, it's time to tackle more sophisticated obedience cues that give vital behavior control.

Teaching Heel:

- Start in a low distraction area and hold a reward at your puppy's nose level, advancing gently as you deliver the "heel" command. Reward each step with you.

- Use an inside turn so the dog brushes your leg as they walk in position. Apply modest leash pressure when needed to keep them close.

- Work up to longer healing times, shifting pace and direction often. Occasionally reward with "breaks" for your pet to smell and release tension.

- Practice heeling in front of mirrors so your puppy can see the desired position.

- Expect setbacks when increasing distractions outside. Reinforce regularly and utilize real-life rewards like getting to greet people or dogs.

- Apply a prompt second cue like "uh uh" or light leash pop if your puppy breaches position, then redirect back to heel and reward. Stay patient!

Teaching Wait:

- With your puppy on a leash, put treats in your closed palm and say "wait" while you extend your hand at a stop signal. Do not let them grasp the treat.

- The second they hesitate or glance at you, indicate the behavior with a click or "yes" and deliver the treat.

- Help your puppy wait for gradually longer durations before treating each time they hesitate on cue.

- Once they comprehend waiting for your hand signal, bring in the verbal "wait" cue and fade the hand signal.

- Increase distance by taking steps back or turning your back as the puppy waits in position for the release cue.

- Proof the habit by making your dog wait while environmental distractions like bouncing balls or unlocked doors pass by. Reinforce the remaining put.

- Use "wait" before doors, street corners, and other critical spots. Do not release until calm and focused.

Teaching Leave It:

- With the dog on a leash, lay a reward on the floor and cover it with your hand while you say "Leave it." Block access to the goodie.

- The moment they quit trying to acquire the goodie, mark by saying "yes!" and provide an alternative reward from your other hand.

- Gradually increase the temptation by utilizing tastier rewards on the floor, dropping treats from standing height, or "accidentally" dropping food during walks. Say "leave it" each time.

- Practice using toys and other items you want your puppy to ignore. Reward them for overcoming temptation.

- Once "leave it" is thoroughly known, start utilizing it as a redirection cue if your puppy tries to grasp anything improper.

Recalls and Emergency Stops

A solid recall and emergency halt are two of the most crucial actions to master with a powerful guardian breed like the Cane Corso. Follow this guidance for training rock-solid responses:

Recalls:

- Start "recall" training on a long leash in a low-distraction area. Say your puppy's name and "come" in an energetic voice while backing up excitedly. Praise and reward when they run to you.

- Increase the recall difficulty progressively by introducing additional distance, distractions, tempting scenarios like approaching people/dogs, and training off-leash in enclosed spaces initially.

- Always praise loudly and give high-value incentives when your puppy comes to you on cue. You want to make coming back highly worthwhile.

- Designate a special "emergency recall" cue that is only used when essential and regularly rewarded with an outstanding treat jackpot. This trigger should stimulate intense attentiveness.

- Avoid repeating your recall cue over and again - say it once then go get your dog if they don't answer right away to reinforce coming when called the first time.

- Periodically practice enjoyable recalls while running backward, tossing rewards, and utilizing toys/squeakers to generate drive for responding. Keep training sessions cheerful.

- Proof your recall in real-world areas like parks. If your Cane Corso brushes you off to run after something, just make a mental note and practice more targeted recalls in that scenario. Stay persistent!

Emergency Stops:

- With your dog in a long line, start racing away from them, then abruptly turn and cry "Stop!" in a forceful tone. The leash pressure should halt your puppy in their tracks. Praise immediately.

- Pair the halt order with an outstretched arm like a stop signal to strengthen the verbal cue. Use an extremely severe tone solely for emergencies.

- Gradually phase out the lengthy line and practice the stop/emergency cue on standard walks. Reinforce every quick response.

- Test the stop command by having assistance hold a tempting toy or food and suddenly sprint away from your approaching leashed dog as you provide your cue.

- For enhanced reliability, teach a "sit" or "down" on cue shortly after your stop command is obeyed. This forces your dog to lock in and focus.

- Don't misuse the emergency halt cue - save it for simulating emergencies or truly critical situations only. You want it to retain maximum authority and meaning.

- Troubleshoot delays in responding by repeating long-line training and utilizing higher-value rewards for quick compliance. Also, avoid repeating the cue continuously - say it once with emphasis.

Fun Tricks for Mental Stimulation

Teaching your intelligent Cane Corso tricks and engaging behaviors gives crucial mental stimulation and develops your overall training bond.

Beneficial Tricks:

Fetch/Retrieve
Teach your puppy to take, hold onto, and return anything placed in their mouth or tossed. This satisfies fetch urge in a regulated manner while encouraging impulse control through "drop it" and recall training. Practice with balls, rope toys, and Frisbees.

Weave Through Legs
With your puppy sitting in front of you, step sideways with one leg and coax them into the

opening with a reward. Mark and reward each time they pass through your legs. Gradually remove the lure until they weave successfully on just the verbal signal. This teaches agility, coordination, and body awareness.

Spin Circles

Hold a lure above your puppy's nose and slowly move it in a circle so they follow the treat in motion and "chase their tail." After a few repetitions, add in a vocal signal like "twirl!" when they start spinning. Remember to mark and reward the movement.

Peekaboo

Have your puppy sit or down, cue a "wait", then place a rag over their face for just a second or two. Remove it while praising and provide a treat. Work up to longer durations buried under towels and blankets. This is ridiculous fun while teaching patience.

Roll Over

With your puppy in a down, coax them onto their side by moving a goodie across their shoulder. Continue luring in an arc over their back while giving a "rollover" cue. When they accomplish the roll fully onto their opposite side, mark and reward.

Crawl

Capture the behavior of crawling by rewarding when your puppy lays down and scoots freely forward. Add a verbal cue after the crawling action is fluent. Useful for low-crawling in tunnels or under obstacles.

Bang Game (Play Dead)

Say "bang" in an excited voice while gently rolling your puppy onto their side/back. Praise and treat. Gradually fade away the physical prompting so they tumble onto their back merely from the "bang" cue as if shot and feigning death.

Nose Target

Touch your puppy's nose to a portable target like a foam noodle end. Click and treat each nose touch. Then switch to aiming stationary targets, gradually increasing distance from them. Useful for agility directionals.

Close Doors

Securely attach a rope to a door handle. Say "shut the door" while you teach the puppy to grip the rope and tug the door closed. Mark and reward each first pull attempt, ramping up to fully closed. Great for polite pawing and mouth skills.

Hand Signals

In addition to vocal cues, train essential behaviors like sit, down, stay, and come using just simple hand signals without speaking. This taps into your dog's body language receptiveness and trains them for signing during walks or distracting locations.

Mental Exercise Benefits:

- Reduces boredom and harmful behaviors
- Provides needed mental stimulation and challenge
- Strengthens human-canine friendship and communication
- Helps drain energy in a focused action
- Reinforces training concepts including targeting and impulse control
- Makes training enjoyable and game-like!

Chapter Seven

Exercise and Activity for Cane Corso

Exercise Requirements

As a powerful working breed intended to manage livestock, the Cane Corso needs intense daily exercise to stay fit and well-behaved.

Activity Level:
- High energy and stamina
- Require at least 60-90 minutes of activity daily
- Enjoy having a job or duty to fulfill

Best Types of Exercise:
- Brisk walking or jogging
- Hiking and outdoor adventures
- Swimming or water activities
- Interactive games like fetch

- Canine sports like agility or nose work

Walking Tips:
- Walks should be brisk-paced and entertaining, not lazy strolls
- Incorporate training repetitions and scent games on walks
- Vary sites and give exploratory sniffing time
- Bring incentive items to reward check-ins

Jogging/Running:
- Wait until growth plates finish at 18-24 months before jogging with your Cane Corso to avoid joint damage
- Slowly build up distance and speed once mature to condition appropriately
• Run on soft surfaces like grass or dirt paths to decrease impact
- Make sure temperatures are cold enough to prevent overheating

Hiking:

- Cane Corsos thrive on trekking and outdoor activity due to their energy

- Build the distance and difficulty level progressively as your dog's fitness level improves

- Bring sufficient water and collapsible bowls to prevent dehydration

- Ensure excellent leash manners and recall before hiking off-leash

Mental Exercise:

- Incorporate mental demands into exercises like obedience exercises or nose work searches

- Learning and problem-solving help tire a Cane Corso out productively

- Practice instructions and skills using real-life rewards like tossing balls or releasing to sniff

Yard Time:

- While healthy, yard exercise alone is not enough for this lively breed

- Monitor time outside when conditions are extremely hot or chilly

- Interactive play is more beneficial than just leaving a Cane Corso alone outside
- Avoid excessive running/zooming on slippery terrain to prevent pulled muscles

Signs of Good Exercise:
- Relaxed facial expressions and body posture
- Resting peacefully after activity bursts
- Interested in training and commands
- Content to chew a long-lasting toy

Signs of Needing More Exercise:
- Hyperactive pacing and restlessness
- Persistent demand barking and attention-seeking
- Destructive chewing or digging
• Jumping up on owners constantly
- Difficulty focusing and settling

Exercise Precautions:
- Careful not to over exercise puppies under 18 months as they are still developing

- Slow down on exceptionally hot, humid days to prevent overheating
- Take care exercising on slick ice to avoid muscular injuries and slips
- Monitor for lameness, limping, or reluctance to move which could suggest pain

Playing and Interacting with Toys

Playing with your Cane Corso provides vital bonding time, mental enrichment, and activity.

Best Interactive Toys:

Tug Toys - Allow supervised tug play to satisfy your Corso's natural grip drive. Use robust rope or canvas toys and establish "drop it" guidelines. Avoid playing tug-of-war activities with your hands or clothing.

Fetch Toys - Play controlled fetch games with balls, flying discs, and other safe fetch toys to tap into your dog's prey drive. Teach solid "drop" and "leave it" cues to manage the game. Vary retrieves to keep it hard.

Chew Toys - Durable chew toys like Kongs, Nylabones, or Yak chews provide mental stimulation and chewing enjoyment when filled with treats. Supervise the use of soft, squeaky toys and avoid rawhides.

Puzzle Toys - Food puzzle toys that involve manipulation with paws or nosing around to remove rewards provide a fantastic cerebral workout. Increase difficulty by hiding little bits of their kibble in different puzzle toys to activate their intellect.

Interactive Toys - Toys you move and wiggle yourself like flirt poles, reward balls, and rope toys enhance your dog's interest in play. Interactive play minimizes boredom. Avoid laser toys which might frustrate dogs.

Nosework Toys - Hide and seek games with scented toys or scatter gifts in the grass to enhance natural scenting skills. Nosework is quite cognitively taxing.

Water Toys - Floating, sinkable, and squeaking water toys keep your Cane Corso happily engaged when playing in the water. Choose safe, non-toxic toys if used for retrieving into the mouth.

Agility Toys - Weave poles, tunnels, balance boards, and fitness hurdles develop athletic and agility skills during play in your yard. Moving their body across obstacles provides mental difficulty.

Safe Toy Rules:
- Avoid small toys or objects that could be ingested
- Monitor the use of squeaky toys - discard them if destroyed
- Remove toys once interest wanes to retain novelty

- Rotate the toy bin weekly so favorites don't get overplayed
- Check labels to guarantee non-toxic materials
- Discard damaged toys immediately
- Never leave puppies unsupervised with any toy

Play Tips:
- Play in short spurts to minimize over-arousal or weariness
- Incorporate training into play like asking for sits and downs
- End play sessions on a positive note while interest is still high
- Structure game rules like waiting patiently, "drop it" indications, and calm taking of toys
- Avoid wrestling or pursuit games which can encourage biting
- Manage toy guarding gently using training like "give" and trade up

Benefits of Play:
- Satisfies natural drives like prey, grasp, and tug

- Strengthens your friendship with pleasant interactions
- Provides vital mental and physical exercise
- Helps reduce negative behaviors from boredom
- Teaches polite play etiquette and biting inhibition

Swimming and Other Fun Activities

In addition to conventional exercise, Cane Corsos flourish when given opportunities to participate in exciting structured activities that challenge their bodies and minds.

Swimming:
- Introduce water gradually using lures, flotation aids, and shallow entrance points
- Allow your Cane Corso to decide the pace and don't force water encounters
- Provide adequate praise and support for all water encounters to build confidence

- Supervise closely, don't let your dog unmonitored near water

- Rinse off with clean water after swimming in ponds/lakes

- Introduce swimming carefully to avoid overexertion if your dog is not conditioned

- Pay attention to indicators of weariness or reluctance to keep swimming

Canine Sports:

Agility - The athletic Cane Corso tends to excel at agility. Early introduction to obstacles like tunnels, jumps, and teeter-totters permits progressive skills development. Look for seminars that focus on relationship building. Proper conditioning is crucial.

Nosework - Challenging a Cane Corso's eager nose by teaching them to seek and signal scented targets taps into their tracking talents. Nosework provides tremendous mental exercise and increases confidence.

Dock Diving - Some Cane Corsos love leaping excitedly into the water off docks or boats at competitive dock diving competitions. Allow them to calmly watch and enter at their speed. Building more strength and confidence is crucial.

Flyball - This fast-paced racing relay where dogs jump hurdles and return balls to unleash a tennis ball launcher suits breeds like the Cane Corso that have strong ball drive. Make sure to enforce regulations against dog aggression at interesting events.

Other Fun Fitness Activities:

Hiking/Backpacking - Cane Corsos thrive when hiking on mountain paths and have the stamina for long-distance endurance. Build up mileage gradually and ensure optimum conditioning.

Biking - Athletic Cane Corsos may run consistently behind adult bicyclists. Use cautious bicycling with puppies, especially on particularly hot days. Begin with modest distances and confirm that your dog is not displaying signs of lameness after sessions.

Swimming - Many Cane Corsos become exceptional swimmers when introduced to water gradually. Provide life jackets until dogs gain confidence. Try dock diving, pool fun, or paddling beside a canoe/kayak.

Agility - Home agility courses with tunnels, low jumps, weave poles, and teeter-totters give fun and challenge. Focus on relationship building and confidence.

Barn Hunt - Barn hunt trials tap into the Cane Corso's excellent scent by tasking them to detect hidden rats in straw bales. Dogs must climb over and through obstacles to reach the concealed scented rats.

Weight Pulling - This job-focused practice allows working breeds to evaluate their strength and stamina by pulling successively heavier weighted carts across short distances. Caution must be required to avoid joint injury.

Overall, variation is crucial. The more ways you can occupy your Cane Corso's body and mind, the better! Activities improve your relationship while giving the required stimulus.

Chapter Eight

Nutrition and Healthcare

Choosing a Quality Dog Food

Selecting the appropriate diet is vital for your Cane Corso's health and longevity. Look for these properties in high-quality dog food:

Ingredients:

- First 2-3 components should be specified entire protein sources like chicken, lamb, fish

- Avoid generic words like "poultry meal" - named meats are better

- Look for nutritious carbohydrates such as brown rice, barley, and sweet potatoes rather than fillers

- Include antioxidant-rich fruits and veggies

- Should contain necessary fatty acids from fish oil, vegetable oils

- No artificial preservatives, colors or flavors

- Contains probiotics and chelated minerals

- Meat or fish listed first, not nonspecific words like "meat meal"

Nutritional Standards:

- Formulated to fulfill AAFCO feeding trial requirements or recommendations

- Calcium and phosphorus levels controlled for large breed pups

- Appropriate calorie density to avoid overfeeding

- Balanced omega 3 and 6 fatty acids

- Optimal calcium-phosphorus ratios for bone growth

- Chelated minerals for bioavailability

Brand Backing:

- Produced by a reputed business with considerable nutrition research

- Manufacturer owns and operates their production facilities

- Rigorous quality control and testing

- Customer service team to address questions

- Health guarantee and satisfaction guarantee

Ingredient Sourcing:

- Detailed information on where ingredients are obtained from

- Manufacturing is done in the United States for quality oversight

- Sustainably harvested fish sources

- Antibiotic-free, humanely raised meats

- No components supplied from China

Allergies and Sensitivities:

- Grain-free and limited ingredient versions available if allergies are suspected

• No artificial additives

- Alternative protein sources including duck, venison, or salmon

- Egg-free recipes may benefit dogs with egg allergies

Carefully reading labels allows you to make informed choices when purchasing quality food. Prioritize meat-focused ingredients, nutritional adequacy, and transparency from recognized brands.

Establishing a Feeding Schedule

Establishing scheduled mealtimes and adequate portions puts your Cane Corso puppy up for lifetime health. Follow these tips:

Puppy Feeding:

- Feed puppy food developed for large breeds until at least 12-18 months old for healthy growth

- Provide 3-4 meals a day for puppies up to 6 months old

- Transition gradually to 2 meals a day from 6 months to 1 year old

- Avoid free feeding, which can lead to rapid growth or obesity

- Use regular meals to forecast toilet times for housetraining

Adult Feeding:

- Feed adult or all life stages food from 1-2 years old onward

- Two meals a day is good for adult Cane Corsos

- Monitor weight and modify portions to maintain desired lean body composition

- Feed at predictable intervals each day, ideally morning and night

- Make sure food satisfies basic nutritional standards

Portion Guidelines:

Puppy daily calories:
- 2 - 4 months old - 1200 kcal
- 4 - 7 months old - 900 kcal
- 7 - 12 months old - 800 kcal

Adult daily calories:
- Intact dogs - 1700-2000 kcal
- Neutered dogs - 1300-1600 kcal

Typical adult serving sizes:
- intact males: 4 - 5 cups

- intact females: 3 - 4 cups
- neutered: 3 - 4 cups

Considerations:

- Portions depend on food calorie density - check label guidelines

- Highly energetic dogs may need somewhat more food

- Use regular bodily condition assessments, not simply appetite, to guide food amounts

- Adjust amounts based on weight, exercise level, age, and health status

- Reduce portions if your dog grows overweight

Feeding Tips:

- Carefully measure out quantities rather than eyeballing

- Avoid unhealthy table scraps and people's food

- Keep water dishes full and clean

- Separate dogs during mealtimes if any resource guarding

- Pick up uneaten food after 15-20 minutes until the next meal

- Weigh out kibble rather than using cup measurements for accuracy

Regularly examine your Cane Corso's bodily condition, weight, and muscle tone and modify feeding amounts accordingly. Follow label advice for optimal portions based on life stage and activity level.

Veterinary Care and Prevention

Establishing a good relationship with your veterinarian ensures your Cane Corso receives optimal preventative care and stays healthy.

Finding a Veterinarian:

- Ask reliable dog owners for vet referrals

- Ensure they have experience with large guardian breeds

- Look for AAHA-accredited veterinary practices

- Meet potential vets in person before committing

- Seek holistic vets if interested in fewer vaccines/medications

- Tour the clinic to assess cleanliness and friendliness

Puppy Exams and Vaccines:

- Exams every 2-4 weeks from 6 weeks to 16 weeks old

- Distemper/parvo combo vaccine starting at 6-8 weeks old with boosters every 2-4 weeks until 16-20 weeks old

- Rabies vaccine is given at 12-16 weeks old depending on the region

Adult Care Schedule:

- Annual wellness exam each year

- Rabies vaccine every 1-3 years depending on vaccine and laws

- Distemper/parvo boosters every 3 years

- Bordetella (kennel cough) vaccination optional annually

- Heartworm test then monthly preventative medicine

- Annual fecal check for intestinal parasites

- Bloodwork as needed to screen for problems

Preventative Care:

- Dental cleanings and daily tooth brushing

- Monthly heartworm prevention

- Monthly flea/tick prevention

- Keep nails clipped to avoid cracking

- Clean ears weekly

- Annual ophthalmologist eye exam

Emergency Preparedness:

- Pet first aid/CPR class and kit

- Pet health insurance or savings fund

- Locate emergency veterinary hospitals

- Obtain emergency contact details and directions to your regular vet

- List of any drugs or pre-existing conditions

- Copies of immunization records

- Recent images of your dog

Maintaining medical records, keeping immunizations up to date, practicing preventive care, and developing a trustworthy veterinarian connection build the foundation for excellent lifelong health.

Chapter Nine

Grooming and Coat Care

Brushing and Deshedding Tools

Frequent brushing and de-shedding keep your Cane Corso's short coat healthy and under control. Use these grooming tools:

Slicker Brush - Metal-wire pinned brushes excel at removing dead hair from the undercoat by penetrating down to the skin. Use mild pressure and avoid scratching the skin.

Undercoat Rake - Double-row undercoat rakes help draw out loose hairs from the undercoat when the Cane Corso is heavily shedding. Use an upward motion to prevent scratching the skin.

Bristle Brush - For general smoothing and distribution of coat oils. Use bristle brushes as a finishing brush after undercoat removal. The delicate tipped bristles glide across the topcoat.

Deshedding Tool - Rubber grooming tools with blunt metal edges pull off a dog's loose undercoat when used properly. The fine teeth catch dead hairs but won't scratch like blades. Move against coat growth direction.

Hound Glove - Use rubber grooming gloves as a gentle alternative to bristle brushes for daily smoothing. The rough rubber nubs gather shed fur.

Shedding Blade - Stainless steel shedding blades with ultra-fine dull edges help peel out dead undercoats on heavy shedding breeds like the Cane Corso. Take care not to apply too much pressure.

Combo Brush - Dual-sided brushes with pin bristles on one side and short metal tines on the other allow you to undercoat the rake and finishing brush in quick succession.

Zoom Groom - Rubber grooming tools with cone-shaped teeth stimulate the skin and generate natural oils. Use them during bathing to work in shampoo.

Lint Brush - Handy lint rollers effortlessly remove dead hair from your home and clothes between full grooming sessions. They immediately catch shed hair and prepare for visitors.

Regularly brushing - Use a slicker or bristle brush regularly to remove dead hairs, distribute coat oils, and prevent tangles or mats. Sensitive body parts may require a very soft brush.

Weekly Deshedding - During seasonal shedding cycles, use an undercoat rake, shedding blade, or de-shedding equipment 1-2 times a week to keep loose hair under control.

Shine Conditioner - After a bath, apply a conditioning product developed to promote coat shine, repel dirt, and prevent tangles. This helps smooth the coat for simpler future brushouts.

Brushing Tips: - Work in portions and brush against the coat growth direction
- Start at the head and go back to the body - Use short, delicate strokes to avoid scratching the skin - Increase brushing time and frequency during shedding seasons
- Always brush dry coats - avoid combing wet hair - Check for mats, knots, or skin lesions when grooming - Reward obedient dogs with food and praise

Benefits of Regular Brushing: - Removes dead and loose hair - Distributes natural oils throughout skin and coat - Prevents mats and tangles - Brings out coat shine - Allows bonding time with your dog -

Helps measure coat and skin health - Decreases the quantity of shedding around home

Regular brushing sessions provide the ideal time to inspect your dog's coat closely for any irregularities or problems between vet visits.

Bathing Techniques

Bathing a Cane Corso too regularly will dry out their skin and strip the coat of oils. Follow these techniques for an efficient bath:

Bathing Frequency:

- Adult Cane Corsos only require thorough bathing every 4-8 weeks

- You can spot clean face, paws, and dirty areas between full washes

- Increase bathing frequency to weekly or bi-weekly at peak shedding seasons

- Avoid very frequent bathing which eliminates protective oils

Bathing Equipment:

- Use a handheld shower sprayer with adjustable pressure

- Invest in an excellent quality dog shampoo and conditioner

- Fill a pitcher with warm water to moisten the face and rinse the eyes

- Purchase a non-slip bath mat for safety and comfort

- Use a hydraulic table to reduce back strain (big dogs)

Pre-Bath Brushing:

- Thoroughly brush the coat before bathing to eliminate dead hair

- Pay additional attention to matting and knots to gradually loosen up

- Clip nails and clean ears out before bathing

Washing Technique:

- Wet your Cane Corso's coat starting at the chest and hind end

- Apply a sufficient amount of shampoo and lather up

- Let shampoo stay for 5-10 minutes before rinsing

- Rinse thoroughly - aiming downwards to avoid ears/eyes

- Repeat shampooing for particularly filthy coats

Drying Technique:

- Squeeze out excess water and pat dry with an absorbent towel

- Use a high-velocity dryer on low heat to blow out the undercoat

- Brush frequently while drying to prevent knots from forming

- Make sure your dog's coat is dry to prevent cooling

Conditioning:

- For enhanced shine and coat health, apply a conditioning spray after bathing

- Ensure skin is dry before applying conditioner products

Clean Face:

- Carefully fill a squeezable bottle with warm water to wet the face

- Mix a tiny amount of dog shampoo in a bowl for face cleaning

- Rinse eyes, beard, and facial folds using the squeeze bottle

- Dry facial hair meticulously to prevent hot places

Nail Clipping and Ear Cleaning

Regular nail trims and ear cleanings are vital components of maintaining your Cane Corso. Here are tips for success:

Nail Trimming:

Nail Clipper Types:

- Scissor clippers - additional leverage for huge, thick nails

- Guillotine clippers - avoid nail splintering with sharp blades

- Grinder - safest option but acclimate dog first

Frequency:

- Trim nails at least every 2-3 weeks for indoor dogs

- Outdoor dogs may need bi-weekly trims if nails don't wear down naturally

Prep:

- Have a styptic powder on hand to halt bleeding if you trim too short

- Give a long-lasting chew reward later for cooperation

• Introduce handling paws early and often

Technique:

- Have a volunteer deliver food regularly to distract your dog

- Hold paw firmly and stretch one toe at a time

- Trim just the sharp point on the white section - prevent pink from fast

- Take little repeated snips to gradually trim the nails

- Give praise and treats for cooperating!

Signs Nails Are Too Long:

- Audible clicking on floors
- Unable to fully extend/contract feet - Irregular posture when the dog moves

Ear Cleaning:

Steps:

- Never push cotton swabs inside the ear canal - clean the outside ear only

- Fill the ear with a veterinarian-approved solution - let soak briefly

- Wipe away trash with cotton balls - repeat until clean

- Dry ears completely after cleaning

Frequency:

- Weekly earwashing helps avoid infections

- Clean daily if ears are inflamed, reddish, or releasing odor

Signs of Ear Trouble:

- Head shaking and scratching at ears

- Visible discharge or debris

- Reddened skin or unpleasant odor

- Swelling, crusting or hair loss

- Reluctance to have ears touched

See your veterinarian soon if these signs develop, since ear infections require medicine. Prevention with frequent cleaning is the greatest medication!

Following a consistent grooming program provides the opportunity to evaluate your Cane Corso for any strange lumps, skin lesions, or areas of pain that demand veterinary treatment. Don't skip these essential grooming duties.

Chapter Ten

Correcting Unwanted Behaviors

Understanding Root Causes

Curing undesired habits in your Cane Corso needs understanding what's causing them. Consider these probable factors:

Lack of Exercise

Pent-up energy and boredom from inadequate activity often emerge as destructive chewing, agitated conduct, or hyperactivity. Make sure your Corso gets at least 60-90 minutes of rigorous daily activity.

Lack of Mental Stimulation

Intelligent but under-challenged Cane Corsos act out with undesired habits. Provide puzzle toys, training games, new experiences, and nose work activities to exercise their minds.

Improper House Training

Dogs won't be adequately alert to go outdoors if they haven't been properly house trained utilizing positive reward and prevention. Revisit toilet training steps if accidents continue.

Attention-Seeking

Cane Corsos will resort to actions like jumping, nipping or stealing prohibited items solely to receive owner interaction and attention. Ignore attention-seeking activities and praise serenity.

Fear and Anxiety

Reactions like aggressiveness or destruction can result from underlying anxiety or lack of healthy socializing. Help timid dogs build confidence through counterconditioning and desensitization.

Separation Distress

Howling, destruction and indoor accidents can ensue when dogs are disturbed when left alone. Implement crate training and separation exercises to combat separation anxiety.

Insufficient Training

Cane Corsos allowed owners to drag owners on a leash, jump on people, or ignore commands that lack proper obedience foundations. Enroll in training sessions and practice daily.

Confusion

Unclear or inconsistent house rules confuse dogs, resulting in them choosing their habits. Set clear boundaries and reward wanted actions consistently.

Changes in Routine or Environment

Big changes like changing homes, having a new baby, or shifting schedules might spark acting out. Help dogs adjust via extra care, training, and environmental control.

Medical Issues

Pain, illness, or disorders like thyroid problems might contribute to rapid behavior changes. Rule out medical reasons with your veterinarian.

Genetic Tendencies

Prey drive, wariness of strangers, or same-sex aggressive tendencies in Cane Corsos must be carefully addressed through rigorous socialization and training.

Adolescent Testing

Cane Corso teenagers from 6 months to 2 years old will naturally challenge limits. Expect some disobedience and manage with more patience and consistency throughout this phase.

To change your dog's undesired behaviors, you must first understand the underlying motivators and triggers. Then you may address the root problem through training, enrichment, and management.

Implementing Positive Reinforcement

Changing undesired habits requires the strategic use of positive reinforcement and wise antecedent control. Follow these steps:

Decide Your Goal Behavior

Choose a specified goal behavior to reinforce instead of the issue behavior. Make sure it's incompatible with the unpleasant action and easy for your dog to offer.

Manage the Environment

Prevent undesirable behavior by restricting access, reducing rewards, and modifying triggers. For example, keep off-limit locations blocked, confine unattended time, and eliminate attractive objects. This sets your dog up to succeed.

Gather Reinforcers

Figure out rewards your specific dog finds extremely motivating such as food treats, toys, play, and the opportunity to smell and greet other dogs. You'll need them to reinforce alternate wanted behaviors. Having a "reinforcer menu" creates diversity.

Capture Alternatives

Watch for times when your dog picks appropriate alternate behaviors on their own instead of the unpleasant habit. Catch those moments and promptly mark them with a "yes!" or click and reinforce them.

Leverage Spontaneity

Reward spontaneous suitable activities before your dog has a chance to conduct the unpleasant activity. For example, when your dog stays settled instead of jumping, reward calmness first. This encourages the good while leaving little possibility for the bad.

Keep Sessions Short

When actively retraining an issue, do multiple short training sessions of just 5-15 repetitions to keep your dog attentive and involved. End each session on a good note leaving your dog wanting more.

Avoid Unintended Reinforcement

Ensure you are not unwittingly rewarding the harmful behavior by giving it attention, especially negative attention. Some dogs regard owner interactions like scolding or shoving them off furniture as worthwhile.

Let Preferred Behaviors Pay Off

Let your dog suffer natural consequences for undesirable behaviors while making the right behaviors genuinely "pay off" with thrilling rewards. For example, hopping up leads to ignoring while four paws on the floor wins attention and treats.

Analyze Progress

Track how frequently the unpleasant conduct occurs day-to-day and week-to-week. An increase in good habits and a decrease in difficulties demonstrate you are on the correct path.

Troubleshoot Plateaus

If progress pauses, review your training plan. Are you offering prizes frequently enough? Are environmental triggers being managed? Is an underlying medical condition at play? Tweak your approach accordingly.

Patience and Positivity!

Some undesired behaviors become deeply established via months of practice. Change won't happen overnight. Stick with good techniques to witness gradual progress over time. Celebrate small successes!

Managing Specific Problems Like Barking

Habitual barking arises from numerous motivations in dogs. Identify the fundamental cause in your Cane Corso to teach quiet:

Barking for Attention

Attention-seeking Cane Corsos learns that barking garners owner contact. Ignore barking totally. Only provide attention when silent. Reward silence with goodies.

Barking from Boredom

Barking that seems to occur in the context of inactivity and under-stimulation implies insufficient exercise or enrichment. Increase regular aerobic exercise, supply food puzzles, and commence training games.

Barking at Noises

Alarm barking at outside sounds often comes from a lack of desensitization. Play ambient outside sound recordings at low volumes during mealtimes. Slowly raise the volume while your dog remains quiet for goodies.

Barking from Stress

Anxious barking due to isolation, changes in habit, or unfamiliar situations requires counterconditioning with praise, toys, and rewards when trigger sounds occur.

Barking at Visitors

Territorial barking at visitors necessitates teaching alternate wanted behaviors for incentives, like sitting for greetings or going to a mat with a long-lasting chew.

Demand Barking

Ignore persistent barking demanding things like food, doors opening, or ball throwing. Wait for peaceful times then reward. Don't reinforce demands with attention.

Barking from Fear

Desensitize and counter-condition dogs to terror triggers that generate terrified barking utilizing extremely slow exposure and high-value food rewards for calm replies. Avoid floods.

Barking at Other Dogs

Teach solid "watch me" cues with high-value goodies. Use this focused eye contact to refocus your dog's attention from other dogs. Maintain reasonable distances from trigger dogs.

Barking in Crate

Make sure needs are satisfied and introduce crating gradually with positive connotations. Provide safe chewing inside the crate. Ignore barking but reward silence.

Barking During Play

Some Cane Corsos vocalize when playing. Redirect to rambunctious play to relax. Allow reasonable play barking as long as it's not excessive.

Designating a very specific alert bark cue like "speak" for treat rewards minimizes issue barking in circumstances where you want your Cane Corso silent and attentive. Be patient – eliminating excessive barking requires consistency.

Chapter Eleven

Living Happily with Your Cane Corso

Establishing Rules and Routines

Cane Corsos thrive when households establish fair, rigid norms and predictable routines. Here are some tips:

House Rules

- Set fundamental house etiquette like no begging, chewing inappropriate stuff, or possession violence over toys/food.

- Designate approved places for your dog vs off-limit rooms. Use baby gates to manage access.

- Train a "go to your bed" cue to send your dog to a corner bed when you need them out from underfoot.

- Teach "leave it" to prevent garbage raiding, stealing food, or snatching prohibited home goods.

- Incorporate frequent "settle" cues throughout the day to encourage relaxation.

Outdoor Rules

- Establish spaces in your yard where your dog can dig and self-entertain. Block off garden beds.

- Decide on play rules like not jumping on someone or mouthing too forcefully. Reinforce the behaviors you want instead.

- Train a firm recall so your dog learns coming when called is non-negotiable, especially while exploring or playing outdoors off-leash in secure places.

- Set up an outdoor tethering system to keep your dog safely confined to a grassy spot when you need to step inside briefly.

- Require courteous leash walking and greetings without pulling or jumping up before letting your dog play in parks.

Routine Schedule

- Feed meals, take walks, and commence playtime/training on a consistent schedule. Routines generate predictability.

- Adhere to regular nap hours crated or secluded from the household action to prevent over-arousal. Puppies need 18+ hours of sleep daily.

- Stick to a regular morning toilet break plan to assist preserve housetraining behaviors.

- Schedule regular weekly grooming and nail trim sessions.

- Always use the same walking route in the neighborhood; dogs relax when they know the path.

- Keep training routine consistent - same cues, same rewards, same class hours.

- Maintain a predictable exercise program - for example, walks on Monday/Wednesday/Fridays and a dog park on Sundays.

- Create a consistent departure procedure when leaving pets short alone - treats in crate, white noise, curtains shut.

Benefits of Structure

- Reduces anxiety and improves security.

- Teaches respect for domestic norms.

- Maximizes learning by repetition.

- Aids in good housetraining.

- Lowers enthusiasm levels.

- Provides mental stimulation.

- Makes problem behavior elimination simpler when rules are apparent.

Balance flexibility with constancy. Sticking to a routine 80% of the time adds security. The occasional deviation won't undermine progress.

Ensuring Proper Socialization

Raising a stable, amiable Cane Corso demands extensive, good experiences with people, dogs, and novel stimuli beginning in puppyhood. Follow this socializing guidance:

Introduce New individuals - Start introducing your Cane Corso puppy to a wide variety of individuals immediately in a calm, positive manner. Go carefully and ensure every interaction is accompanied by incentives and praise. Increase diversity.

Experience locations - Frequently introduce your puppy to new locations like pet stores, parks, and metropolitan settings. Pair novel situations with play and treats to improve confidence. Let your puppy explore at their speed.

Teach Handling - Desensitize your puppy to being touched, handled, and examined with frequent cooperative care like nail trims, teeth brushing, and paw handling. Prevent dread of restriction or manipulation.

Inviting Home Guests - Welcome guests to your home starting in puppyhood so this feels usual. Provide other spaces your Cane Corso can relax in if feeling overwhelmed by guests. Teach them to relax on a mat with a chew.

Dog-to-Dog Mingling - Arrange regular pleasant play sessions with friend's dogs whose immunization history and temperament you trust. Playpen puppy programs promote safe early dog exposure. Require nice greetings.

Counterconditioning - If scared reactions occur during a particular interaction, employ counterconditioning by calmly rewarding with high-value treats any time the trigger comes into view. Use distance to keep your pup under the threshold. Build up extremely slowly over numerous sessions.

Respect Breed Tendencies - Cane Corsos tend to be aloof with strangers and same-sex hostile. Take socializing carefully, foster confidence through enrichment and training, and safeguard your puppy from unfavorable encounters.

Prioritize Social Needs - Make sure your Cane Corso dog gets their vital socializing needs satisfied through regular, carefully regulated contact. This should be a key priority in puppy raising.

Troubleshoot Reactivity - If your teenage or adult Cane Corso exhibits reactivity or aggression on a leash or in the home, seek advice from an experienced trainer/behaviorist using force-free behavior modification. Avoid physical corrections.

Lifelong Social Growth - Socialization is a continuing process during a dog's lifetime. Continue offering your adult Cane Corso with variation in safe, structured situations to preserve skills. Avoid complacency.

Be Proactive - Use the important early developmental windows like 8-12 weeks for the greatest impact. It's far harder to make up for missed socialization later than to do it right the first time.

Proper socialization built over time offers this faithful guardian the confidence and coping abilities to flourish as a reliable companion. Make sociability a habit, not just a puppy class.

Reward-Based Training Tips

Training a Cane Corso should always focus on reinforcing preferred actions using rewards-based strategies. Follow these positive training tips:

Use Food Rewards - Food treats make fantastic motivators to reinforce behaviors you want. Vary rewards to keep it interesting. Gradually cut down food rewards as habits strengthen.

Keep Sessions Short - Limit formal training repetitions to just a few minutes at a time numerous times a day during puppyhood. This ensures sustained growth without tiredness.

Train Before Meals - Your puppy is most ready to work for food rewards when slightly hungry before mealtimes. Make use of this natural food desire.

End on a Positive - Always finish sessions with easy successful repetitions that end on a high note and leave your puppy wanting more at the next session.

Make It Fun! - Training should feel like an enjoyable game to your puppy. Use pleasant praise, diversity, and play rewards to keep energy enthusiastic.

Train Spontaneously - Look for organic occasions in daily life to reinforce actions like sitting, down, or looking at me as they happen organically. Capture and reward smart choices.

Use Life Rewards - Incorporate real-life rewards your dog values naturally like tossing a ball, releasing to greet someone, or getting to go outside. These strengthen behaviors faster.

Prevent Rehearsal - Manage your house and schedule to prevent the puppy from practicing undesired habits like chewing, pottying indoors, or play biting. These are self-reward.

Avoid Flooding - Gradually introduce potentially scary stimuli like loud noises from a distance instead of overpowering the puppy. Go slow enough to keep them quiet.

Clarify Cues - Use the same verbal and hand signal cues consistently each time you ask for a behavior. For example, verbal "sit" accompanied by upward hand gestures. This eliminates confusion.

Respect Attention Spans - Keep training sessions focused yet brief to accommodate puppy attention capacities. Incorporate breaks and play. Increase duration progressively.

Troubleshoot - If your puppy seems to stop growing on a skill, examine how you are motivating and rewarding. Increase value and variety of rewards.

Prevent Rehearsal - Manage the surroundings during down periods to avoid your puppy rehearsing undesired habits like destruction, accidents, or demand barking in your absence.

Patience! - Some abilities like strong recall, loose leash walking, or extended stays take months of incremental growth across numerous situations and contexts. Persistence pays off.

Make sure all family members keep to the same reward-based approach. Force-free training develops mutual trust and greater behavior comprehension. Stay positive!

20 homemade food recipes ideas for Cane Corso with ingredients and preparation instructions

1. Chicken and Rice Delight

Ingredients:
- 2 cups cooked chicken, shredded
- 1 cup brown rice, cooked
- 1/2 cup carrots, coarsely chopped
- 1/2 cup peas
- 1 tablespoon olive oil

Instructions:
1. In a pan, sauté carrots and peas in olive oil until soft.
2. Mix cooked chicken, rice, and sautéed veggies.
3. Allow it to cool before serving your Cane Corso.

2. Beef and Sweet Potato Stew

Ingredients:

- 1 pound lean ground beef

- 1 cup sweet potatoes, diced

- 1/2 cup green beans, chopped

- 1 cup beef broth

Instructions:

1. Brown ground beef in a pot, then drain excess fat.

2. Add sweet potatoes, green beans, and beef broth.

3. Simmer until vegetables are tender. Let it cool before serving.

3. Salmon and Quinoa Feast

Ingredients:

- 1 cup cooked salmon, flaked

- 1/2 cup quinoa, cooked

- 1/4 cup spinach, coarsely chopped

- 1 tablespoon coconut oil

Instructions:

1. Mix flakes of salmon, cooked quinoa, and chopped spinach.

2. Add melted coconut oil and stir until thoroughly blended.

3. Serve at room temperature.

4. Turkey and Pumpkin Casserole

Ingredients:
- 1 pound ground turkey
- 1 cup pumpkin puree
- 1/2 cup blueberries
- 1 tablespoon flaxseed oil

Instructions:

1. Cook ground turkey until browned, then drain.

2. Mix in pumpkin puree, blueberries, and flaxseed oil.

3. Allow it to cool before offering it to your Cane Corso.

5. Vegetarian Delight with Lentils

Ingredients:

- 1 cup lentils, cooked

- 1/2 cup carrots, diced

- 1/2 cup broccoli, coarsely chopped

- 2 tablespoons olive oil

Instructions:

1. Sauté carrots and broccoli in olive oil until soft.

2. Mix cooked lentils with sautéed vegetables.

3. Let it cool down before serving.

6. Turkey and Brown Rice Medley

Ingredients:

- 1 cup ground turkey, cooked

- 1 cup brown rice, cooked

- 1/2 cup peas

- 1/4 cup carrots, grated

- 1 tablespoon fish oil

Instructions:

1. Combine cooked ground turkey, brown rice, peas, and grated carrots.

2. Add fish oil and stir well.

3. Let it cool before serving.

7. Pork and Apple Bites

Ingredients:

- 1 cup pork, cooked and diced
- 1/2 cup apples, coarsely chopped
- 1/4 cup green beans, sliced
- 1 tablespoon olive oil

Instructions:

1. Sauté diced pork, chopped apples, and sliced green beans in olive oil.

2. Allow the mixture to cool before serving it to your pet friend.

8. Chicken and Pumpkin Stew

Ingredients:

- 2 cups chicken, cooked and shredded

- 1 cup pumpkin, diced

- 1/2 cup carrots, sliced

- 1 cup chicken broth

Instructions:

1. Combine shredded chicken, chopped pumpkin, sliced carrots, and chicken broth in a pot.
2. Simmer until vegetables are soft.
3. Cool before serving.

9. Venison with Sweet Potato Surprise

Ingredients:

- 1 cup venison, cooked and shredded

- 1 cup sweet potatoes, mashed

- 1/4 cup blueberries

- 1 tablespoon coconut oil

Instructions:

1. Mix shredded venison, mashed sweet potatoes, and blueberries.

2. Add melted coconut oil and stir well.

3. Serve at room temperature.

10. Salmon and Oat Delicacy

Ingredients:

- 1 cup canned salmon, drained
- 1/2 cup oats, cooked
- 1/4 cup carrots, coarsely chopped
- 1 tablespoon flaxseed oil

Instructions:

1. Combine drained salmon, cooked oats, and diced carrots.

2. Add flaxseed oil and blend completely.

3. Allow it to cool before offering it to your Cane Corso.

11. Duck and Potato Casserole

Ingredients:

- 1 cup duck meat, cooked and shredded
- 1 cup potatoes, chopped and boiled
- 1/4 cup green peas
- 1 tablespoon olive oil

Instructions:

1. Sauté shredded duck, cooked potatoes, and green peas in olive oil.
2. Let it cool before serving.

12. Sardine and Carrot Delight

Ingredients:

- 1 can sardine in water, drained
- 1/2 cup carrots, grated
- 1/4 cup spinach, coarsely chopped
- 1 tablespoon fish oil

Instructions:

1. Mash drained sardines and blend with grated carrots and chopped spinach.

2. Add fish oil and mix until thoroughly incorporated.

3. Serve at room temperature.

13. Lamb and Rice Pilaf

Ingredients:

- 1 cup ground lamb, cooked

- 1 cup white rice, cooked

- 1/2 cup zucchini, diced

- 1 tablespoon coconut oil

Instructions:

1. Brown ground lamb in a pan, then mix with cooked rice and diced zucchini.

2. Add melted coconut oil and mix completely.

3. Allow it to cool before serving.

14. Chicken Liver and Quinoa Bowl

Ingredients:

- 1 cup chicken liver, boiled and chopped

- 1/2 cup quinoa, cooked
- 1/4 cup peas
- 1 tablespoon olive oil

Instructions:
1. Sauté chopped chicken liver, cooked quinoa, and peas in olive oil.
2. Let the mixture cool before serving.

15. Turkey Bacon and Sweet Pea Pasta

Ingredients:
- 1 cup turkey bacon, cooked and crumbled
- 1 cup whole wheat pasta, cooked
- 1/2 cup sweet peas
- 1 tablespoon fish oil

Instructions:
1. Mix crumbled turkey bacon, cooked pasta, and sweet peas.
2. Add fish oil and mix until thoroughly incorporated.

3. Serve at room temperature.

16. Buffalo and Pumpkin Stew

Ingredients:
- 1 cup ground buffalo meat, cooked
- 1 cup pumpkin, diced
- 1/2 cup green beans, sliced
- 1 cup beef broth

Instructions:
1. Cook ground buffalo meat until browned, then add diced pumpkin and sliced green beans.
2. Pour in beef broth and boil until vegetables are soft.
3. Cool before serving.

17. Tuna and Brown Rice Medley

Ingredients:
- 1 can tuna in water, drained
- 1 cup brown rice, cooked

- 1/4 cup carrots, finely chopped

- 1 tablespoon olive oil

Instructions:

1. Mash drained tuna and add it with cooked brown rice and diced carrots.

2. Add olive oil and blend well.

3. Serve at room temperature.

18. Venison and Blueberry Bowl

Ingredients:

- 1 cup venison, cooked and shredded

- 1/2 cup blueberries

- 1/4 cup sweet potatoes, mashed

- 1 tablespoon coconut oil

Instructions:

1. Mix shredded venison, blueberries, and mashed sweet potatoes.

2. Incorporate melted coconut oil and mix completely.

3. Allow it to cool before giving.

19. Chicken Hearts and Spinach Casserole

Ingredients:
- 1 cup chicken hearts, cooked and chopped
- 1/2 cup spinach, finely chopped
- 1/4 cup carrots, grated
- 1 tablespoon fish oil

Instructions:
1. Combine chopped chicken hearts, chopped spinach, and grated carrots.
2. Add fish oil and stir well.
3. Serve at room temperature.

20. Pork Liver and Barley Delight

Ingredients:
- 1 cup pork liver, boiled and diced
- 1/2 cup barley, cooked
- 1/4 cup peas

- 1 tablespoon olive oil

Instructions:

1. Sauté chopped pork liver, boiled barley, and peas in olive oil.

2. Let it cool before serving it to your furry buddy.